Grandpa, I have a VERY IMPORTANT question!

Is Santa Real?

Grandpa, I have a VERY IMPORTANT question!!!

Copyright © 2025 Lou Pappas

All rights reserved.

No part of this publication may be reproduced, distributed or transmitted in any form, or by any means, including photocopying, recording or other electronic or mechanical methods, without the prior written permission of the publisher, except in the case of brief quotations embodied in reviews and certain other noncommercial uses permitted by copyright law.

The moral right of the author and illustrator has been asserted.

Story and Illustrations by: Lou Pappas

Published by: Lou Pappas
loupappas52@gmail.com

Design and Editing: Chris Stead, Old Mate Media
www.oldmatemedia.com

ISBN Paperback: 978-1-922740-28-1
ISBN Hardcover: 978-1-922740-29-8
ISBN Digital: 978-1-922740-30-4

Dedication

This book is dedicated to my Greek Grandpa who is the kindest, most generous person I've ever known.

Dilly was anxious. Just like last **Christmas**, she was still pondering an important question. One that all the other big kids in her class were very curious about, too.

Today, Dilly was visiting her Grandpa and it was time to find out the answer once and for all. She raced to the front door and eagerly began knocking.

"**Sooooooo**, who is 'we?'" Grandpa asked, as Dilly marched into the living room.

"All the big kids," she explained, raising her arms to help make her point.

Grandpa let out his typical "**hummmmmm**," sound. The one he makes when he is thinking. Finally, he reached for an old book from the top shelf. "Come in and let's start from the beginning.

"Long ago there lived a kind, Greek Bishop named St. Nicholas and..." Grandpa started.

Grandpa grinned and said in a soft tone, "you're right, it's total fantasy. You may be a big girl now, but the little ones love the magical tale of a flying reindeer."

Dilly paused to think. She was feeling good about her progress, but still had other concerns.

"Ok, what about going down a fireplace? That's silly! **Bacon** and **Beans** would never allow it. Plus, eating all those cookies would make Santa sick."

"Well, aren't you smart! "You're right, going down a fireplace is silly," Grandpa said, "but St. Nicholas was known to deliver gifts in unusual ways. He also traveled with his helper Billy, and we know how much goats can eat."

Dilly liked being called smart, but her mind had already begun to wander as she nervously paced back and forth. Suddenly she asked in a cracked voice, "what about the naughty or nice list?

THAT'S SO SCARY!"

Grandpa shook his head sternly:

"NO!"

"St. Nicholas would never scare a child."

After a brief smile, a sense of sadness washed over Dilly's face. "So, while these are nice stories, there's no real proof that Santa is real."

"Well just wait one second,"

all the forest friends demanded. "Let's look at the facts."

"In fact, it all starts on December sixth. That's when we celebrate the **Feast of St. Nicholas**. The day **God** spreads the spirit of kindness around the world.

"Then, throughout December and January, people continue to celebrate their religion by focusing on...

LOVE,

KINDNESS

AND

RENEWAL."

As he gathered his thoughts, Grandpa took a deep breath and grumbled, "back in 1931, St. Nicholas received a makeover."

"He got a new look and a new name. His home was moved to a secret location at the North Pole.

His goat Billy became a reindeer called Rudolph. And his forest friends were described more like kids making toys.

DOES THAT SOUND FAMILIAR?"

He smiled as he could see Dilly following along. After shooing away the cat, Grandpa went on: "Despite these changes, the spirit of **St. Nicholas** shines bright. Every year people find kindness in their hearts, bringing joy to so many."

Grandpa looked into Dilly's eyes and said something that warmed her heart "Dilly, I've witnessed several acts of kindness from you this year."

Do you remember last **Christmas**?" A huge grin quickly spread its way between Dilly's ears. "Of course," she declared. "I gave everyone a note with a special message? I see the one I gave you in that book!"

"That's right," Grandpa confirmed. "I remember a lot of happy tears. It was the best gift ever! But how did it make you feel?

"Oh Grandpa,"

Dilly replied, "it was magical. I felt like a glowstick beaming…

with Love."

For several heartbeats the room went quiet with the crackling fire the only sound. Suddenly, Dilly leapt to her feet and spurted out, "I get it!"

"When you receive the gift of kindness from St. Nicholas, you want to pass it on again and again and that gift comes from the real Santa. The spirit inside!"

"No act of kindness, no matter how small, is ever wasted."

— Aesop

About the Author

Grandpa Lou Pappas is a 73-year-old living some of the best years of his life. Prior to retirement there was never enough time to fully engage in art. Now that retirement has come, he enjoys spending time learning, practicing and producing art.

After winning a juried art contest with a project that included a handwritten short story, he became inspired to write and illustrate his first children's book. Lou feels so fortunate to work with Chris Stead of Old Mate Media, who helped a computer-challenged grandpa edit and assemble his book.

Picking a subject to write about was easy, as Lou thought about the many interactions with his grandchildren. One stood out more than the others with a subject that is near and dear to his heart.

Children are open, honest and sincere. Being a good listener and allowing the child to work through their concerns is always a winning strategy.

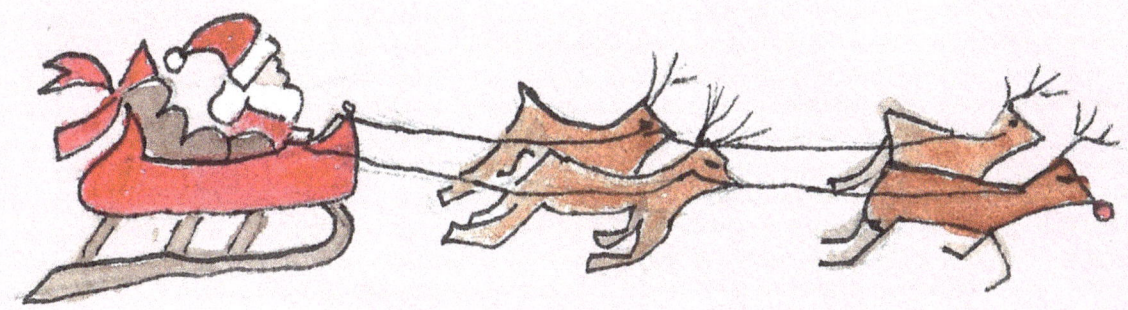

www.ingramcontent.com/pod-product-compliance
Lightning Source LLC
Chambersburg PA
CBHW041216240426
43661CB00012B/1058